Tennis

Marshall Cavendish
Benchmark
New York

This edition first published in 2010 in North America by Marshall Cavendish Benchmark

Marshall Cavendish Benchmark
99 White Plains Road
Tarrytown, NY 10591
www.marshallcavendish.us

Published in 2009 by Evans Publishing Ltd, 2A Portman Mansions, Chiltern St, London W1U 6NR

Editor: Nicola Edwards
Designer: D.R. Ink
All photographs by Wishlist except for page 6 © 2007 Getty Images; page 9 © Bongarts/Getty Images;
page 12 © 2007 Getty Images; page 13 © 2008 Getty Images; page 22 © 2007 Getty Images; page 23
© 2008 Getty Images; 81800297; page 26 Popperfoto/Getty Images; page 27 © Getty Images 2008/AFP

Library of Congress Cataloging-in-Publication Data

Gifford, Clive.
 Tennis/by Clive Gifford.
    p. cm. — (Tell me about sports)
 Includes index.
 Summary: "An introduction to tennis, including techniques, rules, and the training regimen of
 professional athletes in the sport"—Provided by publisher.
 ISBN 978-0-7614-4463-3
 1. Tennis—Juvenile literature. I. Title.
 GV996.5.G55 2009
 796.342—dc22
                                    2008049020

Marshall Cavendish Editor: Megan Comerford

Printed in China.
135642

The author and publisher would like to thank Tom Paine, Emily Louise Robinson, Andrew Love,
Gemma Trodd, Gleanne Purcell, James Heathcote, Brian Heathcote (Coach), and the Rugby Tennis Club
for their help in making this book.

Contents

Tell Me About . . .

Tennis	6
Game, Set, and Match	8
The Court and Gear	10
Star Players	12
Forehand Strokes	14
Backhand Strokes	16
Serving and Receiving	18
Near the Net	20
Movement and Tactics	22
Tennis Rules . . . OK!	24
The World of Tennis	26
Where Next?	28
Tennis Words	29
Index	30

Tennis

▲
French tennis star Gael Monfils reaches for a ball during a crucial tournament match. Top players are great athletes.

Tennis is an action-packed sport for two or four people. A two-player game is called a singles match. A game with four players (two per side) is called doubles. Players use a racket to hit a tennis ball around an area called a **court**. There are different ways of hitting the ball. These are called shots or strokes.

Tennis was once seen as a gentle pastime played by ladies in chic dresses and men in jackets. But now it is a dramatic and exciting sport where players move with great speed and hit spectacular, powerful shots.

You can start playing tennis at any age. Young players may play a version called Mini or Kanga Tennis. It is played on a smaller court with a ball that bounces high, giving new players more time to hit the ball.

The four players move in close to the net during an exciting game of doubles. When you play doubles you need to work well with your partner. Playing both doubles and singles will help you improve as a tennis player.

A junior tennis racket and tennis balls are not very expensive. It is a good idea to get advice on buying the right size racket for you.

Tennis is great fun to play after school with your friends. Many young players decide to take things further and play in junior competitions. There, they get to push themselves to their limits and test out their shots. One day, they may even get to play in famous tournaments just like the stars.

To become a good tennis player, you must practice as often as you can. Even if you're on your own, you can practice your shots against a wall, away from a road. Tennis lessons with a coach are a great way to improve how you play.

Game, Set, and Match

▼ This player has forced his opponent to hit a high-arcing lob. He can now hit a strong shot called an overhead smash. A good smash sends the ball quickly out of the opponent's reach to win a point.

▶ If you hit the ball into the net and it doesn't land on the other half of the court, you lose the point.

In a tennis match players win points by forcing their opponent to make a mistake or by hitting a shot into a part of the court that their opponent cannot reach.

A point starts when a player throws the ball up in the air and hits it to an opponent. This is called a **serve**. If a player serves the ball correctly and the other player hits it back, a **rally** begins. The two players move around the court hitting the ball. The point continues until one player hits a shot past the other player or makes a mistake.

The ball is only allowed to bounce once on your side of the court. If it bounces more than once you lose the point.

◄ The scoreboard shows that the players have won two games each in the third set and have one point each in the fifth game of that set. Pete Sampras (pictured) has won the first two sets.

Tennis has a unusual way of scoring. In tennis, 'love' means zero points. Look at the panel on the right. The first player to win four points (which are scored 15, 30, 40, and game) wins the game, unless the scores are tied at 40-40, or **deuce**. Then, one player has to win two points in a row to win the game.

A set is made up of a number of games. The first person to win six or seven games and be two or more games ahead of his or her opponent wins the set. There is no time limit. The first player to win two or three sets usually wins the match!

Game Scoring

Here is an example of how a game of tennis is scored:

Player A	Player B	Score
1 point	0 point	(15-love)
2 points	0 point	(30-love)
2 points	1 point	(30-15)
3 points	1 point	(40-15)
4 points	1 point	(Game Player A)

Marathon Matches

● In a 2004 men's match, Fabrice Santoro and Arnaud Clement took a record 6 hours and 33 minutes to finish.

● At Wimbledon in 1969, Pancho Gonzalez and Charlie Pasarell played a match that went on for 112 games before Gonzalez won.

● Rob Peterson and Ray Miller played a single rally for over nine hours in 2001. They hit an incredible 17,062 strokes!

The Court and Gear

Tennis is played on a rectangular court divided into two halves by a net. The edges of the court are marked with thick white lines—sidelines at the side and **baselines** at each end. A tennis ball is 'in' if it bounces on any part of the line. If you hit the ball and it lands outside the sideline or baseline then it is 'out' and you lose the point.

A Tennis Court

A tennis court measures 76 feet (23.77 m) long and 36 feet (10.97 m) wide.

Net

The small rectangles within the court close to the net are called service boxes.

Service line

Sideline for singles

Baseline

Sideline for doubles

The sidelines are narrower for singles matches and wider for doubles. The space between these two sidelines is nicknamed the tramline.

The net stands 3 feet (91 cm) high in the middle and a little higher at the side where it is fixed to posts. Your tennis shots have to clear this net. If the ball clips the net and drops onto the other side of the court during play, it is considered still in play and the point continues.

You will run around the court a lot during a game so it is vital that your sneakers are really comfortable. They must fit well and offer good grip on the court. Thick sports socks help soak up sweat and keep you from getting blisters.

The rest of your tennis clothing should also be comfortable and loose enough for you to move your arms and legs freely. Cotton T-shirts and shorts or a sports skirt are ideal. Many players wear sweatbands on their wrists as well.

Grass and Clay

In 2007, Roger Federer and Rafael Nadal played a match on a court which had one half made of clay and the other made of grass!

Many top players have a favorite type of court. Rafael Nadal loves clay courts. He won 81 matches in a row on clay between 2005 and 2007.

▲ This player is waiting to receive the ball from her opponent. She is well dressed for tennis in a skirt, tank top, and sneakers.

Star Players

▲ Roger Federer signs some autographs for young fans. Federer is famous for his politeness off court as well as his great skill on it.

Professional tennis players live exciting lives. Many of them become millionaires from prize money won at tournaments. Some companies pay tennis stars to advertise their products, such as tennis rackets and clothing. The top professionals fly all over the world and, wherever they go, they are cheered on by thousands of fans.

Away from the noise and bustle of a major tournament, tennis players have to live a disciplined life. They eat a healthy diet and work hard on their fitness as well as practicing their shots.

Almost all top players work with their coach every day. They may practice for as long as five or six hours a day on court.

Federer Facts

By May 2008, Roger Federer had won over $39.9 million in prize money from tennis tournaments, the most ever won by any player.

Federer has won the famous Wimbledon tournament five times in a row. The only other man to do this is Bjorn Borg.

The professional tennis season is very long. It starts in January and lasts until November. Professional players are expected to behave well toward fans and officials even when they lose matches or are struggling to play well.

Training hard and playing dozens of matches can place great strains on a player's body. Many players suffer injuries. They then have to work really hard to regain their fitness.

▼ Spanish tennis star Rafael Nadal practices a two-handed backhand shot while his coach watches.

Forehand Strokes

Shots in tennis are divided into backhand and forehand shots. Backhand shots are where you reach across your body with the racket. You make forehand shots on the same side as your racket arm. So, if you hold your racket in your right hand, forehand shots are to your right and backhand shots to your left.

The most common forehand shot is called the forehand drive. Play this shot after the ball has bounced on your side of the court. Aim to use a smooth, relaxed swing to send the ball back low over the net.

▲ A coach will show you a good, comfortable racket **grip** for forehand shots and backhand shots. You alter your grip for different shots.

▼ This player hits a good forehand shot with a long swing. See how her racket ends up in a high position.

Twist your waist and swing your racket back so that your front shoulder (your left shoulder if the racket is in your right hand) is pointing toward your target. Then, as the ball arrives, turn your waist and swing the racket forward.

Aim to hit the ball just in front and to the side of your body. The ideal height to hit the ball is between the knee and just above waist height.

Players try to get in a good position nice and early so that they have time to play their shot. This is not always possible to do, so players also learn to stretch high or reach low to hit the ball at different heights.

▶ Your arm carries on swinging through after you've hit the ball. After you've played your shot, stay alert and move for your next shot.

Backhand Strokes

You play backhand shots on the side of the body opposite that used to make forehand shots. Many new players find these shots harder to perfect, but they are really important to learn. Having a good backhand and forehand allows you to play shots on both sides of your body.

The most common backhand stroke is the backhand drive. Watch the ball as it flies toward you and get into a good position. Aim to hit the ball between knee and waist height.

▼ Sometimes you have to hit the ball when it is lower or higher than you would like.

▲ Here, a player makes a backhand volley. His racket meets the ball just in front of his body.

Turn your shoulders to bring your racket back. Then swing your arm forward from the shoulder. Keep your wrist strong and firm as you hit the ball. Your racket keeps on swinging forward after you've hit the ball.

Some players prefer to use two hands on their backhand shot. Both hands grip the racket and the player can then swing through the ball using strength from both arms. In this way players can hit the ball with a little more power.

◄

Coaching can really help improve all your shots, including your backhand.

Serving and Receiving

A tennis match starts when one player serves the ball and continues until the first game is won or lost. Then the other player serves a game, and so on. A serve is hit overhead but when young players are starting out, some of them may choose to use an underhand serve.

There are many serving rules. Both your feet have to be behind the baseline as you serve. You toss the ball up into the air and have to hit it into the service box that is diagonally opposite.

If the ball's first bounce isn't inside the correct service box, the **umpire** will signal a fault. Luckily, you get a second chance to serve. If this is also a fault, a **double-fault** is called and you lose the point.

▼ The first serve of a game is aimed into the left service box. For the next point, the server stands to the left of the middle of the court and aims the ball into the right service box.

The serve can be a good weapon. Top players hit fast and tricky serves into the corners of the service box. These are hard to return. To win a game when the other player is serving is called a break of serve.

A player receiving the ball has little time to react. He or she must judge which direction the serve will travel and what shot to play to send the ball back. If the player receiving the ball misses it completely, the server is said to have hit an **ace**.

Super Serves

Top male players can hit serves at over 125 mph (200 km/h). Andy Roddick holds the world record with an amazing serve of 152.8 mph (246 km/h).

Female players aren't far behind either. In 2007, Venus Williams hit a serve that reached 127 mph (204 km/h).

Two players have hit 51 aces in a single tennis match—Joachim Johansson and Ivo Karlovic. Both feats occurred in 2005 and despite all those aces, both players lost their matches!

▼ A serve starts with the player standing sideways to the net. The ball is thrown up high and the racket brought over to hit the ball with the arm almost stretched. The racket is angled down a little to send the ball down into the service box.

Near the Net

Sometimes, you will get the chance to race toward the net. This is an attacking move. Your next shot is likely to be a **volley**. This means you will hit the ball before it bounces on your side of the court.

You don't need a big swing of the racket when making volleys. Instead, you hit the ball with a short, sharp punch. For this you need to keep your wrist firm as the ball and racket meet.

Not at the Net

You must not touch the net with your racket or any part of your body or you lose the point.

The last thing you want to do is fall over the net. This happened to Rafael Nadal in practice in 2004 and he had to miss a big tournament because he was injured.

Another net-jumping incident that went wrong was in 1987. Ecuador's Danny Carrera tried to leap over the net after a match but tripped and broke his leg.

◄

This player makes a good forehand volley. She is in the ideal position, about two paces away from the net.

You can make forehand and backhand volleys. You can also bend at the knees and get down low to play a low volley or reach up high to make a high volley. With all volleys, you must try to aim the ball away from your opponent.

If your opponent rushes to the net for a volley, don't panic. Try not only to hit the ball as hard as you can. Aim to hit the ball out of your opponent's reach down the sidelines.

The **lob** is a special stroke that you can use against a player at the net. You hit the ball high enough to pass out of their reach, but so that it lands in the court behind them.

▲ The player on the right has approached the net. His shot was easy to reach for the player on the left, who has hit the ball out of reach down the sideline.

Movement and Tactics

▲
In a good ready position you should stand on the balls of your feet. Your knees should be bent a little with your feet apart. Hold your racket in front of you, but be ready to move it to your forehand or backhand side.

Once a rally starts, you have to think hard and move fast. After playing each shot, try to move quickly to get back into a good position, ready for your next shot.

Some players like to run in toward the net after their serve and hit the ball on the volley, trying to win the point. Others prefer to stay around the baseline and play long, patient rallies, looking for an opening.

Players try to not get caught standing still, especially halfway between the net and the baseline. This area is called no man's land and it makes it easier for your opponent to beat you with a good shot.

When playing your shots, try to move your opponent around the court. A big gap might appear. If you aim your next shot at the

gap, your opponent might not be able to reach it.

When you rest between games, try to think about how the match is going. Have you spotted a weakness in how your opponent plays? Many players prefer their backhand or forehand side. Try to hit the ball where your opponent least wants it to go.

◀

Mario Ancic leaps high to hit an attempted lob by his opponent. He will aim the ball out of his opponent's reach to try to win the point.

▼ You need quick reactions to reach surprising shots by your opponent. Here, this player has sprinted and stretched to reach the ball just in time.

Tennis Rules . . . OK!

A competitive tennis match is run by an umpire. He or she is helped by people called line judges, who watch carefully to see if the ball lands in or out. There is also a net-cord judge who signals whether a ball touches the net on a serve.

The umpire controls the game and his or her decisions are final. This official can issue warnings if a player loses his or her temper, is rude, or breaks another rule such as jumping over the net or smashing a ball away into the crowd. The umpire can award points or games to the opposing player as a punishment.

Tie-Breaks

If the score in a set reaches 6-6, the umpire signals a **tie-break**. This is a way of ending a set quickly. The first player serves for one point, then after that, each player serves for two points. This continues until one player wins the set by reaching seven or more points and having at least two more points than his or her opponent.

◄

This official is called a net-cord judge. The net-cord judge checks to see whether the ball touches the net during a serve. If it does, this is called a let and the player is allowed to serve again.

Apart from the rules of tennis, there is something called etiquette. This is all about showing respect to your opponent and to the officials and anyone watching the game.

Etiquette includes important things such as never arguing, hitting spare tennis balls back to the server gently, and only serving when your opponent is ready.

▲ In competitive matches, the tennis balls are changed regularly. Players who are about to serve with new balls hold them up to let their opponent know.

If you are playing on a row of tennis courts, it also means not getting in the way of other matches. Say you're sorry if your ball lands on another court and wait until a point is over before going to collect it.

▼ Even if you're disappointed at losing, always congratulate your opponents and shake their hands at the end of the game.

The World of Tennis

Top tennis professionals come from all over the world. They play all over the world, too. Tournaments are held as part of tours on every continent. Some players compete at a different tournament every single week of the tennis season.

The top men's tour is called the ATP tour and the top women's tour is called the WTA tour. Players are given ranking points for winning or doing well in tournaments on the tour. These points count toward a player's world ranking. Players with a high world ranking enter the biggest tournaments without playing qualifying matches.

▼

In this Wimbledon doubles match, Venus Williams (*right*) is close to the net. Her sister, Serena, is in support behind her.

The four biggest tennis competitions are the Australian Open, the French Open, the U.S. Open, and Wimbledon. Winning one of these is now called winning a **grand slam tournament**. These four big tournaments have competitions for singles, men's doubles, women's doubles, and mixed doubles. Tennis is an Olympic sport, too.

Most tennis events are for individuals or for doubles pairs. The Fed Cup for women and the Davis Cup for men are team events where a series of games are played against another country.

Match Facts

John Pius Boland won the men's singles at the very first modern Olympics. He had planned to attend as a spectator but was entered by a friend!

The last person to win all four grand slams in a year was German Steffi Graf in 1988. She also won an Olympic gold to complete a memorable year.

The United States is the most successful country in team tennis with 17 Fed Cup wins and 32 Davis Cup wins.

▼ Andy Murray plays a backhand during the 2008 U.S. Open.

Where Next?

Here are some websites and books to help you find out more about tennis.

Websites

http://sports.espn.go.com/sports/tennis/index
This website has news about the latest tennis tournaments and the top professional players.

http://www.ontennis.com/
A website with everything from the rules to the legends of the sport.

http://www.wimbledon.org
Learn all about the famous Wimbledon tournament at the official website.

Books

Williams, Serena, and Venus Williams. *How to Play Tennis.* New York: DK Publishing, Inc., 2004.

Crossingham, John, and Bobbie Kalman. *Tennis in Action* (Sports in Action). New York: Crabtree Publishing, 2002.

Tennis Words

ace A serve that the opposing player is unable to reach and return with his or her racket.

baseline The back line of the court that marks the court's length.

court The place where a tennis match is played.

deuce When the score is 40-40 in a game.

double-fault A mistake when a server fails with two serves in a row and loses the point.

grand slam tournament One of the four big tournaments—Wimbledon, the U.S. Open, the French Open, and the Australian Open.

grip The way that you hold your tennis racket.

lob A high shot played over an opponent and into the court behind.

rally A number of shots made by players hitting the ball to each other.

serve The overhead shot used to start a point in tennis.

tie-break A system used in many tennis matches to end a set after the scores are tied at six games each.

umpire The person who takes charge of a tennis match.

volley A shot in which you hit the ball before it bounces on your side of the court.

Index

Numbers in **bold** refer to pictures.

ace, 19
Ancic, Mario, **23**

backhand, 14, 16, **16**, 17, **17**, 21, 23
ball, 6, 7, 8, 14, 15, 16, 17, 18, 19, 20, 21, 23, 24, 25
baseline, 10, 18, 22
break of serve, 19

coaching, **7**, 12, **13**, **17**
competitions, 7, 25, 26
court, 6, 8, 10, 11, 12, 14, 20, 21, 22, 25

deuce, 9
double-fault, 18
doubles, 6, 10, **12**, **26**, 27

etiquette, 25, **25**

fans, 12, **12**, 13
fault, 18
Federer, Roger, 11, **12**
fitness, 12, 13
forehand, 14, **14**, 15, **15**, 16, **20**, 21, 23

gear, 10, 11
Graf, Steffi, 27
grip, 14, **14**

injuries, 13

let, 24
line judge, 24
lob, 21

Monfils, Gael, **6**
Murray, Andy, **27**

Nadal, Rafael, 11, **13**
net, **8**, 10, **10**, 11, 14, **19**, 20, **20**, 21, **21**, 22, 24
net-cord judge, **24**
new balls, **25**

officials, 13, 24

playing a let, **24**
practice, 12
professionals, 12, 13, 26

racket, 6, 7, 14, 15, 17, 22
rally, 8, 22
ranking, 26
ready position, 22, **22**
rules, 24, 25

Sampras, Pete, **9**
scoring, 9, **9**
service boxes, **10**, 18, 19
serving, 8, 18, **18**, 19, **19**, 22, 24
shots, 6, 7, 8, 11, 12, 14, 20, 22, 23
sidelines, 10, 11, 21
singles, 6, 10, **11**, 27
smash, **8**

tie-break, 24
tournaments, 7, 12, 26
tramlines, 11

umpire, 18, 24

volley, **17**, 20, **20**

Williams, Serena, **26**
Williams, Venus, 19, **26**